MONUMENTAL MILESTONES
GREAT EVENTS OF MODERN TIMES

The McCarthy Era

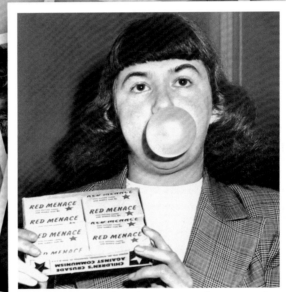

Businesses took advantage of communist fears by promoting pro-American products, such as Red Menace gum.

Mitchell Lane
PUBLISHERS

P.O. Box 196
Hockessin, Delaware 19707

Titles in the Series

MONUMENTAL MILESTONES
GREAT EVENTS OF MODERN TIMES

The McCarthy Era

Senator Joseph McCarthy's obsessive pursuit of communists ruined thousands of innocent lives before destroying his own political career.

Kathleen Tracy

Copyright © 2009 by Mitchell Lane Publishers, Inc. All rights reserved. No part of this book may be reproduced without written permission from the publisher. Printed and bound in the United States of America.

Printing   1   2   3   4   5   6   7   8   9

Library of Congress Cataloging-in-Publication Data
Tracy, Kathleen.
  The McCarthy era / by Kathleen Tracy.
    p. cm. — (Monumental milestones)
  Includes bibliographical references and index.
  ISBN 978-1-58415-694-9 (library bound)
  1. Anti-communist movements—United States—History—20th century—Juvenile literature. 2. Internal security—United States—History—20th century—Juvenile literature. 3. United States—History—1933–1945—Juvenile literature. 4. United States—History—1945–1953—Juvenile literature. 5. United States—Politics and government—1933–1953—Juvenile literature. 6. McCarthy, Joseph, 1908–1957—Juvenile literature. 7. Legislators—United States—Biography—Juvenile literature. 8. United States. Congress. Senate—Biography—Juvenile literature. I. Title.
  E743.5.T73 2008
  973.91—dc22

                                                    2008020929

ABOUT THE AUTHOR: Kathleen Tracy has been a journalist for over twenty years. Her writing has been featured in magazines including *The Toronto Star*'s "Star Week," *A&E Biography* magazine, *KidScreen* and *TV Times*. She is also the author of numerous books for Mitchell Lane Publishers, including *William Hewlett: Pioneer of the Computer Age; The Fall of the Berlin Wall; Leonardo da Vinci; The Story of September 11, 2001; Johnny Depp; Mariah Carey;* and *Kelly Clarkson*.

PUBLISHER'S NOTE: This story is based on the author's extensive research, which she believes to be accurate. Documentation of such research is contained on page 46.

The internet sites referenced herein were active as of the publication date. Due to the fleeting nature of some web sites, we cannot guarantee they will all be active when you are reading this book.

Contents

The McCarthy Era

Kathleen Tracy

*For Your Information

IS THIS TOMORROW

AMERICA UNDER COMMUNISM!

From the end of World War II until the mid-1950s, the United States was gripped by a fear of communism often referred to as the Red Scare.

As the Soviet Union emerged as the primary communist power, many Americans were fearful of spies infiltrating the U.S. government and potentially overthrowing its democracy. Media helped perpetuate the fear through magazines presenting sensational headlines and stories about the evils of communism.

The Hollywood Ten

The years following World War II should have been the best of times. America was at peace. Jobs were plentiful, and the country was prospering. But it was also a time of fear and mistrust. Although the Allies had defeated Adolf Hitler's Nazis, a new, insidious enemy had emerged—communists. To most Americans, communism was more than a political and economic ideology; it was a threat to the fundamental freedoms that defined their very way of life. And it seemed to be spreading unchecked across the globe.

The Soviet Union, ally of the United States during World War II, was now a hostile Cold War foe, intent on incorporating its Eastern European neighbors into its sphere of influence. China had already been "lost" to communism when Mao Ze-dong became leader, as had North Korea. Among citizens and politicians alike, there was a genuine fear that communists would try to infiltrate the United States government to undermine America's democracy. There was also concern that communists in the arts would use popular media to spread their message and attract new followers.

"America emerged victorious from the Second World War, both economically and morally the leader of the world. But somehow it got caught by a panic that suddenly resulted in a witch hunt,"[1] Giora Bernstein, founding musical director of the Colorado Music Festival, noted during a 1989 symposium he organized called "Culture and the Red Scare." In 1955, as a young Israeli student at Juilliard, Bernstein was required to swear under oath that he was neither a Nazi nor a communist. He had to report to his visa officer five times a year.

Under this perception of communist encroachment, the House Un-American Activities Committee, or HUAC, began investigating the Hollywood motion picture industry in September 1947. Forty-three people were put on the HUAC witness list. The majority were expected to be "friendly" witnesses, including Walt Disney and future president Ronald Reagan. These witnesses intimated, or suggested, that communists were infiltrating Hollywood in order to infuse movies with Red propaganda.

Nineteen of the witnesses were expected to be "unfriendly" because they had, either in the past or currently, been members of the American Communist Party. They indicated they would not answer questions before the committee, including the crucial, "Are you now or have you ever been a member of the Communist Party?"

It is important to note that membership in the Communist Party was not then, nor has it ever been, illegal in the United States.

Of the nineteen unfriendly witnesses, eleven were called to testify. Only playwright Bertolt Brecht answered the questions posed by the committee. Afterward, he immediately left the United States and returned to Germany.

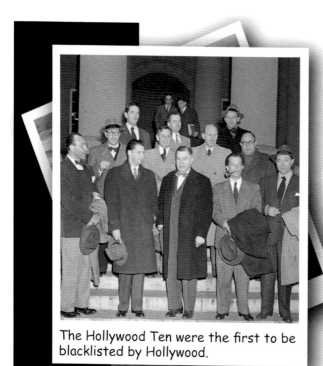

The Hollywood Ten were the first to be blacklisted by Hollywood.

They included one director (Edward Dmytryk) and nine screenwriters (Herbert Biberman, Albert Maltz, Lester Cole, Dalton Trumbo, John Howard Lawson, Alvah Bessie, Samuel Ornitz, Ring Lardner Jr. and Adrian Scott)—all of whom refused to answer HUAC's questions.

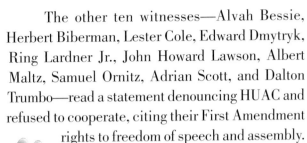

The other ten witnesses—Alvah Bessie, Herbert Biberman, Lester Cole, Edward Dmytryk, Ring Lardner Jr., John Howard Lawson, Albert Maltz, Samuel Ornitz, Adrian Scott, and Dalton Trumbo—read a statement denouncing HUAC and refused to cooperate, citing their First Amendment rights to freedom of speech and assembly. The hearings' chairman, J. Parnell Thomas, ordered them removed from the room by armed guards.

Several well-known Hollywood celebrities, including director John Huston and actors Gene Kelly, Humphrey Bogart, and Lauren Bacall, organized the Committee for the First Amendment, or CFA. They traveled to Washington, D.C., and protested the government's targeting of their industry and rallied to support the Hollywood Ten. They soon backed down as their involvement threatened to damage their own careers.

Humphrey Bogart

In November the Hollywood Ten were officially charged with contempt of Congress. It wasn't long before the film industry turned their backs on the Ten as well.

When the first subpoenas had been sent out, the Motion Picture Association of America, or MPAA, denounced the action. But after the Hollywood Ten were cited for contempt, the film industry backtracked. On November 24, 1947, fifty studio executives—and many of their financial backers—convened in New York City at the Waldorf-Astoria Hotel for a private meeting. Fearing negative publicity and not wanting to take on the federal government, the executives, acting under the authority of the MPAA, agreed to ban the screenwriters. The only way back in would be for the writer to declare under oath that he was not a communist.

The next day, on November 25, Hollywood announced that no communists or other subversives would be employed by the motion picture industry. The industry had officially established a blacklist.

This announcement became known as the Waldorf Statement. By issuing it, and by sacrificing the Hollywood Ten, the studio executives hoped to put an end to HUAC's scrutiny of the industry.

By 1950, every member of the Hollywood Ten was in jail. Despite the Waldorf Statement, HUAC continued to probe Hollywood. In 1951, a new round of hearings began. This time the issue wasn't so much film content; this time HUAC was aiming for individuals. One hundred and ten witnesses were subpoenaed, and the committee demanded names. It wasn't just a matter of naming people who had openly expressed communist beliefs: HUAC wanted people who might have left-wing views or who might be or have been sympathetic to communists. With HUAC, no proof was needed, just innuendo. And from that innuendo, Hollywood added names to its blacklist. On June 22, 1950, a pamphlet called "Red Channels" was distributed. It named 151 entertainment industry professionals as "Red Fascists and their sympathizers." These names were also added to the blacklist.

Even though it was film career suicide, hundreds of people refused to name names to HUAC, and the blacklist grew to over 300. Included were Stella Adler, Charlie Chaplin, Dashiell Hammett, Burl Ives, Orson Welles, and Arthur Miller. Actress Lee Grant was blacklisted for refusing to implicate her husband.

Having learned a lesson from the Hollywood Ten, uncooperative witnesses invoked the Fifth Amendment—the Constitutional right against self-incrimination—which also protected them from contempt of Congress charges. But it didn't protect their careers. Actor Howard Da Silva, despite having appeared in over forty movies, was blacklisted from the film industry for twelve years. Screenwriter Frederic I. Rinaldo, who had worked on thirty-four movies, and actress Karen Morley, with forty-five screen credits over the course of a twenty-year career, would never work in Hollywood again.

But many did name names over the course of the hearings, including actor Lee J. Cobb, screenwriter Budd Schulberg, and director Elia Kazan. In many cases, the person testifying did at some point have a communist association. Elia Kazan, for example, briefly belonged to the American Communist Party before becoming disillusioned with their ideology and renouncing the group. The HUAC wanted to know who else in Kazan's circle of theater friends had attended meetings. At first, Kazan refused to answer. But after the president of 20th Century Fox studios threatened that Kazan would never work in Hollywood again, Kazan contacted HUAC and gave them what they wanted, identifying eight former colleagues. Although others in the industry named names, Kazan became the poster child for betrayal, in part because of his defiant, unapologetic stance afterward. In all, approximately 324 people were named and subsequently blacklisted.

Along with the blacklist was a less official "gray list." These people were never named by the HUAC, but they were considered unemployable because they had either been friends with a communist, had at some point signed a petition deemed to be subversive, or was simply rumored to have Red leanings. For some people, it was a case of mistaken identity. Regardless, more careers and lives were ruined. The gray lists were compiled by two American Legion magazines, *Firing Line and American Legion Magazine,* that set themselves up as keepers of Democracy.

Even though the HUAC hearings had failed to turn up any evidence that Hollywood was secretly disseminating communist propaganda, the film industry remained gun-shy. Seemingly innocent productions, such as a film about Hiawatha, were scrapped out of fear they could be construed as anti–Cold War movies. Since so many of the top writers had been blacklisted, the quality of films suffered. Business being business, a screenplay black market evolved. According to the book *Red Scare,* "The writers worked for a fraction of their former fees and were denied the screen credit, but it did put food on the table. Over the next decade, aging veterans of the blacklist began making their way in Hollywood once more. But these were the minority. For every one who found the way back, ten or twenty were irretrievably lost."[2]

Colorado screenwriter Dalton Trumbo with his wife, Cleo, at the House Un-American Activities Committee hearings in 1947.

After Dalton Trumbo spent 11 months in jail, he moved to Mexico. Writing under the pseudonym Robert Rich, he wrote 30 scripts and won a Best Screenplay Academy Award for The Brave One *in 1957. In the 1960s, he was reinstated into the Writers' Guild, signaling the end of the blacklist.*

In an ironic twist that was deeply embarrassing to the studio execs, in 1957 the film *The Brave One* won an Oscar for Best Screenplay. The listed writer was Robert Rich, but everyone in the industry knew Rich was a front for Dalton Trumbo. Three years later, Trumbo would receive his first screen credit—for *Spartacus*—in over twelve years. He would go on to write the films *Exodus, Lonely Are the Brave, Johnny Got His Gun,* and *Papillon.* Trumbo was finally officially presented with his *Brave One* Academy Award on May 2, 1975, a year before his death.

Now the blacklist is considered one of the most shameful chapters in American history—a time when careers, and in many cases lives, were ruined by rumor and innuendo. The fear of communism that prompted the acceptance of blacklists and political persecutions was also the avenue for an ambitious young politician from Wisconsin to make a national name for himself. And in the end, Joseph McCarthy would ironically also become a victim of his anti-communism obsession.

FYInfo

FOR YOUR INFORMATION

After World War II, the Allies divided Germany into four zones, each of which would be occupied by one of the four main Allies—Britain, France, the United States, or the Soviet Union. Berlin, the German capital, would also be divided into four sections. The agreement to divide Berlin equally among the Allies put the capital in a strange position: It was isolated within the Soviet zone.

Flag of the Soviet Union

The situation with the Soviets was uneasy. The Western Allies in general and the United States in particular were concerned that communism was gaining support in Eastern Europe and that the Soviets appeared ready to use that support to their postwar advantage. During a speech at Westminster College in Fulton, Missouri, in 1946, Winston Churchill lamented how the Soviets had isolated their satellite countries of Eastern Europe from the West: "An Iron Curtain has descended across the continent. Behind that line lie all of the capitals of the ancient states of central and eastern Europe . . . all these famous cities and the populations around lie in what I must call the Soviet sphere and all are subject . . . to a very high and in some cases increasing measure of control from Moscow."[3]

Joseph Stalin

Soviet leader Joseph Stalin responded angrily in a subsequent speech. He claimed that secure borders—with likeminded communist countries—kept their people safer. "The Soviet Union's loss of life [during World War II] has been several times greater than that of Britain and the United States of America put together. . . . And so what can be so surprising about the fact that the Soviet Union, anxious for its future safety, is trying to see to it that governments loyal in their attitude to the Soviet Union should exist in these countries?"[4]

This was the beginning of what would be known as the Cold War: an unarmed conflict pitting the ideals of democracy against those of communism that would last for the next fifty years.

Senator Joe McCarthy, July

Even as a youth, McCarthy was ambitious. He dropped out of school and started his own business. He later earned his high school diploma by finishing four years' curriculum in nine months.

Early Years

Joseph Raymond McCarthy was born on November 14, 1908, in the Irish farming community of Grand Chute, Wisconsin. The fifth of seven siblings, Joe grew up in an eight-room, white clapboard house on his family's struggling 140-acre farm, located a hundred miles north of Milwaukee. His parents, Timothy and Bridget, were loving but strict and expected their children to help with chores almost from the time they could walk.

Stocky with a barrel chest, short arms, and thick legs, Joe was teased mercilessly by his older brothers. Shy about his appearance, he would often hide when neighbors came over to visit. Because of his awkwardness, Bridget was especially protective of Joe, and would constantly tell him he was going to be special when he grew up.

Joe attended the Underhill School, a one-room schoolhouse. Blessed with a sharp mind and quick intellect, the lessons bored him. At fourteen, after completing eighth grade, Joe dropped out of school and went to work on his father's farm. He quickly tired of that, too, so he started his own business raising chickens. Initially the business prospered, but after disease wiped out his flock, Joe went to work at a grocery store in nearby Appleton. Even though just nineteen, Joe showed the ambition that would characterize his life, and he was soon named store manager. He was then transferred to manage a new store in Manawa, thirty-five miles away. He packed his few belongings into an old truck and left to start a new life.

Joe quickly earned a reputation as a young man with boundless energy. Naturally competitive, he was constantly on the go and sought out strenuous activities to challenge himself. "Joe was steamed up when he came to Manawa," a friend later recalled. "I never saw anybody so steamed up. He just couldn't ever relax; he worked at everything he did. He was pushing all the time."[1]

Working at the grocery store allowed Joe to meet many people. He enjoyed discussing local issues with men his own age, but he soon felt his lack of education would seriously handicap his plans to advance in life. Joe decided to go back to school. He attended Little Wolf High School, and in just nine months earned his high school diploma. In 1930,

Little Wolf High School

he enrolled at Marquette University, intending to become an engineer. Although he had to work part-time jobs to support himself, he participated in extracurricular school activities, including boxing and student government.

In elementary school, Joe had never played sports. "He was too rough and couldn't work with the team," a former classmate later recalled. "And he couldn't seem to learn the rules."[2]

On the boxing team, Joe was known for being aggressive, if not particularly skilled. Although he managed to overwhelm some opponents with a barrage of wildly thrown punches, he also took some painful beatings when he came up against someone who had good boxing skills. But even then he seemed to savor the competition.

As a senior he ran for class president against Charles Curran, who had previously defeated Joe for debating club president. To show they were both good sports, McCarthy and Curran promised during their campaign that they would vote for each other. The first vote ended in a tie. Curran suggested they cut a deck of cards to decide the winner. Joe insisted the class vote again. This time, McCarthy won by two votes, meaning only one person had changed his ballot. When Curran asked Joe if he had gone back on his word and voted for himself, McCarthy said, "Sure. . . . You wanted me to vote for the best man, didn't you?"[3]

Two years into his studies, Joe switched to law. He earned his law degree in 1935 and opened a private practice in Waupaca. Business was so slow he had to support himself by playing poker in the backroom of the local tavern.

The other regulars complained that Joe took all the fun out of the game because he was so intense.

By this time, Joe had developed an interest in politics. He joined every civic group he qualified for and introduced himself to as many people as he could. A proud Democrat, McCarthy was elected president of the Young Democrats of the Seventh District of Wisconsin. In 1936, he ran for district attorney but was soundly beaten. The setback made him reassess his political affiliation.

A short time later, McCarthy was offered a job with a law firm in Shawano. Even though the job paid him a weekly salary, he was still always broke because he was a compulsive spender. His job at the law firm paid him $200 a week, a comfortable sum, especially for a single man, but he was constantly asking for advances on the next month's salary. His employer tried to help by withholding a percentage of his paycheck so that he would have some savings, but McCarthy always ended up needing it.

The owner of his law firm was Mike Eberlein, a well-known Republican who had lost elections for both state attorney general and U.S. senator. Eberlein's latest goal was to become a circuit court judge. Before he could announce his candidacy, Eberlein was stunned to discover his associate had beat him to it. Joe left the practice soon after.

Few people would have given McCarthy much of a chance. For one thing, he was just thirty years old, and his law experience was minimal. But what McCarthy lacked in legal ability and court savvy he made up with inexhaustible energy and burning ambition. He canvassed the region, stopping in every town, regardless how small. He talked to everyone and anyone. He charmed housewives and engaged their husbands in conversation. He empathized with the plights of both farmers and businessmen. He also distorted the truth when necessary.

Joe's opponent was Judge Edgar V. Werner. McCarthy suggested that the jurist, then sixty-six, was too old to serve, repeatedly misrepresenting Werner's age as seventy-three. He also intimated that the judge had been cheating the public by earning up to $200,000 during his time on the bench. He didn't mention that Werner had served thirty-five years, so his actual average salary was under $6,000 a year.

Judge McCarthy in his office at the Outagamie County Courthouse in 1946.

In his 1939 campaign for circuit court judge, McCarthy displayed the hard-ball tactics for which he would later become nationally notorious.

The damage was done. McCarthy handily beat Judge Werner and in 1939 became the youngest circuit court judge in Wisconsin history. He wasted no time displaying his signature intensity. Joe inherited a backlog of 250 cases on his judicial calendar. To catch up, he worked overtime, keeping his court in session until past midnight on a dozen different occasions. Once his calendar was cleared, he volunteered his services in other districts. Beneath his Herculean work ethic was an ulterior motive—McCarthy already had his sights set on running for the U.S. Senate.

By using the tradition of exchanging benches with other Wisconsin judges, McCarthy was able to travel the state and ingratiate himself with local politicos and build relationships with newspaper reporters. He also cemented his reputation as a decisive, efficient jurist. He was known to decide divorces within five minutes. But there was a darker side to Judge McCarthy that was a harbinger of controversies to come.

McCarthy was a circuit court judge, which means he presided over trials. Municipal courts typically handle lesser offenses such as traffic infractions, juvenile violations such as truancy and missing curfew, and small claims. Circuit courts are where criminal proceedings and civil matters such as divorce are litigated.

Unlike today when state courts are highly regulated by legislative statutes, in the 1930s the court system was sometimes like the Wild West. Wisconsin, where McCarthy presided, was typical. "There was no uniformity among the counties. Different types of courts in a single county had overlapping jurisdiction, and procedure in the various courts was not the same. A number of special courts sprang up in heavily urbanized areas . . . many municipalities established police justice courts for enforcement of local ordinances, and there were some 1,800 justices of the peace."[4] Plus, when compared to modern jurists, there was relatively little oversight of the judges. This lack of oversight is one reason why McCarthy was able to run his courtroom pretty much any way he wanted to.

But his hard-line mentality needs to be seen in the context of the times. In the 1930s, America was struggling through the Great Depression and a national crime wave. Millions of people were out of work and in desperation turned to crime—both as individuals and as organized mobs. It was the era of notorious bank robbers such as John Dillinger, Bonnie and Clyde, Baby Face Nelson, and Pretty Boy Floyd. Public Enemy #1 was a crime boss named Al Capone. Being a hard-nosed judge and tough on crime and criminals was something the public wanted and appreciated.

Bonnie and Clyde

Originally, the term *circuit court* referred to a court that moved. Judges would travel to different locations within the court's jurisdiction to oversee cases. During the nineteenth century, judges traveled on horseback, often with a group of lawyers. Abraham Lincoln rode the circuit in Illinois as a young attorney. As cities emerged, permanent courts replaced the "circuits," although the term *circuit court* remained.

Judge McCarthy in June 1942, shortly [...]
took a leave of absence from his judic[...]
joined the U.S. Marine Corps.

After the attack on Pearl Harbor, Judge McCarthy made arrangements to join the U.S. Marine Corps as a commissioned officer.

Political Ambitions

McCarthy had grown used to dispensing his own brand of justice without much outside interference, but the Quaker Dairy case brought both scrutiny and reprimand. Dairy farmers in the Appleton area of Wisconsin complained that Quaker Dairy was undercutting the prices it paid for their milk, a practice illegal under state statute. Finally, the Wisconsin Department of Agriculture intervened and sought an injunction, or a court order, to prevent further price cutting.

McCarthy waited six weeks before holding a hearing on the matter. During that delay, Quaker Dairy had hired an outside attorney to assist their in-house counsel. That lawyer just happened to be a good friend of Judge McCarthy. After initially granting the Department of Agriculture's request for an injunction, McCarthy reversed himself and revoked it. Then, in his final ruling, he determined that Quaker Dairy had in fact violated the state's price-cutting law, but he also ruled that since the statute was scheduled to expire in six months, there was no point in forcing the company to adhere to the law because it would be an undue hardship on the company. McCarthy dismissed the case.

The Department of Agriculture's attorney, Gilbert Lappley, was stunned and furious. He demanded a trial but McCarthy declined, saying it would be a waste of the court's time. Lappley appealed McCarthy's decision to the State Supreme Court in Madison. The justices were equally disturbed. They wrote: "We are cited no authority and we find none which justifies a court suspending the operation of a statute on the ground that it will work a hardship if it is enforced. It must be concluded that the grounds on which the trial court acted did not constitute a sufficient or proper legal reason therefore and that this action constituted an abuse of judicial power."[1]

When the state justices asked for a copy of the court transcript to document exactly what had transpired, McCarthy informed them he had directed the court stenographer to destroy his notes because in his opinion they were not material, or legally important. The Wisconsin Supreme Court issued a stinging rebuke of McCarthy.

"Ordering destruction of these notes was highly improper. . . . We can only say that if it were necessary to a decision, the destruction of evidence under these circumstances would be open to the inference that the evidence destroyed contained statements of fact contrary to the position taken by the person destroying the evidence."[2]

When the justices ordered the original injunction against Quaker Dairy to be reinstated, McCarthy had no choice but to comply. During the trial, however, McCarthy took out his ire on Lappley, bitterly admonishing him in open court. Lappley stood his ground in face of McCarthy's inappropriate tirade. The attorney knew that if he walked out, McCarthy could charge him with contempt—the one judicial power for which there is no appeal to a higher court.

When Lappley tried to secure a transcript of McCarthy's remarks, it was not available. Soon after, he began to get letters and phone calls criticizing him for causing McCarthy trouble with the state supreme court. When Lappley attempted to defend himself, he was pressured to drop the issue. Lappley felt the public had a right to know what had happened and refused—so he was fired. News of Lappley's dismissal was kept out of the papers, as McCarthy's network of friends and cronies circled the political wagons. Lappley was the first of many who would discover how dangerous it could be to cross Joseph McCarthy. Being a judge was simply the first step in his long-range plan of moving into national politics. Everything he did in his professional life could be seen as a calculated move to achieve that goal, and he would run over anyone who got in his way.

On December 7, 1941, the Japanese bombed Pearl Harbor and hurtled the United States into World War II. As a sitting judge, McCarthy was automatically deferred from the draft. But in early June the following year, Judge McCarthy wrote a letter to the U.S. Marine Corps recruiting officer in Milwaukee and negotiated an officer's commission if he enlisted. Afterward, he gave an interview to the *Milwaukee Journal*, in which he claimed he was resigning from

During his military service, McCarthy worked as an intelligence officer. Although he liked to call himself Tail-Gunner Joe, he never actually fired a weapon in combat.

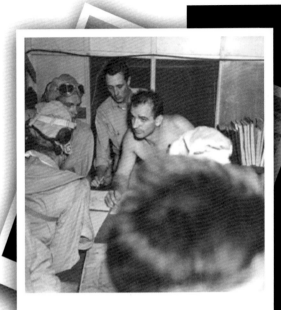

Captain McCarthy briefing pilots in 1943.

his $8,000-a-year judgeship and enlisting as a private out of a sense of patriotism. However, as he had arranged, McCarthy was sworn in as a first lieutenant. He wore his uniform to court on his last day before leaving for basic training at Quantico in Virginia. In fact, he had not resigned but had taken a leave of absence.

McCarthy served in the Pacific as an intelligence officer in the Marine Air Unit. His preoccupation remained politics, and he never missed an opportunity to promote himself. He once arranged a photo session with the Associated Press showing him seated in the rear of an inactive dive-bomber shooting off a round of ammunition, intimating he was a tail gunner, which he was not. After breaking his leg falling down the stairs on an aircraft carrier, McCarthy told people he had been wounded in action, a story that was published in his hometown newspaper.

By early 1944 McCarthy had decided to run for Wisconsin's Republican senatorial nomination. Although he had been a Democrat earlier in his public life, Wisconsin was a heavily Republican state, so he stood a better chance of getting elected by switching political parties. While stationed at Bougainville in the Solomon Islands, McCarthy began campaigning, putting signs that read McCarthy for Senator in the windows of military jeeps and trucks.

McCarthy was granted a leave from the Marine Corps in July and returned to Wisconsin to campaign against Republican incumbent Alexander Wiley in the primary. He got around the military regulation that forbade any enlisted soldier from speaking publicly on political issues by starting his speeches by saying, "If I weren't in uniform, I would say . . ."[3] He also defied the Wisconsin constitution prohibiting members of the state judiciary from holding any other public office during the term for which they were elected. Although he ran a competitive campaign, earning 80,000 votes, McCarthy lost to Wiley and in August returned to active duty at the Marine Corps Air Station in El Centro, California.

When he was denied another leave a few months later, McCarthy resigned and was relieved from active duty in April 1945 with an honorable discharge. "Tail Gunner" Joe returned home a war hero. He won reelection to the circuit court by a wide margin but was already planning his next senatorial run.

In 1946, McCarthy narrowly defeated incumbent Robert La Follette Jr. in the Republican primary. In the general election he garnered twice as many votes as his Democratic challenger. Joseph McCarthy was finally on his way to Washington as the new junior senator from Wisconsin.

After losing an election as a Democrat in 1944, McCarthy was a surprise winner against longtime Senator Robert La Follette Jr. in the 1946 Republican primary.

At 7:48 A.M., on December 7, 1941, three hundred and fifty Japanese warplanes attacked Pearl Harbor, Hawaii, where half of the U.S. Navy's Pacific Fleet was anchored. A second wave of warplanes struck after 8:30. By 10:00 A.M., it was over. In all, 2,403 Americans were killed, and 188 planes and eight battleships were either destroyed or badly damaged. Despite the horrible losses, the attack had not taken out the Pacific Fleet. All the aircraft carriers had been out to sea, the submarines

Bombers from the USS *Hornet* fly over a burning Japanese cruiser during the Battle of Midway.

had survived virtually intact, and Pearl Harbor itself was still usable. Although the U.S. Navy was temporarily crippled, it would recover. The United States had no choice but to declare war on Japan.

Because of the damage inflicted by the attack on Pearl Harbor, it took a while for the United States to seriously challenge Japan's hold on the Pacific. But in 1942, after U.S. intelligence officers deciphered Japan's secret code, they intercepted a message that the Japanese fleet was headed for Midway Island. In a bold move, most of the U.S. fleet was deployed to defend the tiny island. The U.S. victory at Midway, in which the U.S. sank 4 of Japan's 6 aircraft carriers, was a turning point in the war of the Pacific.

Slowly over the next three years, U.S. forces gained control of the western Pacific, island by island, using both ground forces and bombing raids by Marine pilots—the kinds of missions in which McCarthy participated. The fighting came to a head at Iwo Jima, 650 miles from the mainland of Japan. More Marines—110,000 transported on 880 ships—were sent into this battle than any other, which began February 19, 1945. For 36 days the Marines engaged in battle against over twenty thousand Japanese defenders entrenched in the island's terrain. In the end almost 7,000 U.S. Marines died, making it the bloodiest battle in the history of the Corps. Nearly all the Japanese defenders died in the fighting. Five months later, after the bombing of Hiroshima and Nagasaki, the Japanese surrendered, and the war was over.

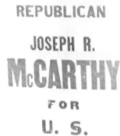

U.S. Senator Joe McCarthy stands be
campaign posters in 1946. Between 1
McCarthy spearheaded investigation
communist influences in the U.S. gove

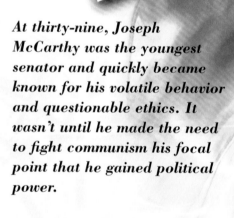

At thirty-nine, Joseph McCarthy was the youngest senator and quickly became known for his volatile behavior and questionable ethics. It wasn't until he made the need to fight communism his focal point that he gained political power.

National Exposure

Joseph McCarthy was just thirty-nine when he took office in 1947, making him the youngest United States Senator. However, to drive that point home, he shaved a year off his age in his official biography, claiming he was born in 1909. He sought to present himself as a young maverick.

According to friend and adversary alike, Joseph McCarthy was a likable man. He could be charming and engaging, companionably putting his arm around people as he talked to them. On the other hand, he had a vicious, unpredictable temper that would flare at imagined slights and insults. When angry, McCarthy was verbally abusive, attacking people personally. As his reputation of being a loose cannon spread, many people began steering clear of the volatile junior senator.

During his first years in Washington, McCarthy did little to distinguish himself as a lawmaker. He still approached politics the way he always had: as a means to an end. And that end was power and prestige. On a national stage, the stakes were much higher and the potential financial gain greater. From 1947 to 1949, for example McCarthy accepted $20,000 from Pepsi-Cola to help the company circumvent the postwar sugar rationing.

He also received $10,000 from members of the prefabricated housing industry. After McCarthy joined the Senate Housing Committee, he spoke out against public housing for veterans. Instead, he promoted the benefits of prefabricated homes, suggesting these were a far superior alternative. Although at the time nobody paid attention to McCarthy's unethical wheeling and dealing, it would come back later to haunt him.

McCarthy entered the U.S. Senate the same year the HUAC began investigating the film industry. The House Un-American Activities Committee was originally established in May 1938. Chaired by Martin Dies, the committee's mandate in those prewar years was to investigate German-American association with Nazis and activity by the Ku Klux Klan. Little if anything was ever done to curb Klan activities, and some HUAC members justified the lack of oversight by saying the Klan was an old American institution. Foreign-born citizens and residents, however, did not enjoy the same consideration.

On June 29, 1940, Congress had passed the Alien Registration Act, making it illegal for any citizen or resident to call for the overthrow of the U.S. government. It also required all alien residents in the United States over fourteen years of age to provide a written statement of their political beliefs. The main target of the Alien Registration Act was the American Communist Party. At that point, it was decided that HUAC would be the best investigative tool to discern whether anyone was trying to overthrow the U.S. government.

In 1945, HUAC was made a permanent committee and given unique powers of subpoena. The majority of Americans initially supported the committee's actions, believing its intimidation tactics were necessary, especially in light of two infamous trials initiated by HUAC's investigations.

The first case involved a U.S. State Department official named Alger Hiss, who up to then had an unblemished record. A Baltimore, Maryland, native, Hiss graduated from Harvard Law School in 1929 and was appointed private secretary to Supreme Court Justice Oliver Wendell Holmes for one year. Afterward Hiss worked briefly at a Boston law firm before getting a job with a firm in New York City. In 1933 he received a telegram from his old law school professor, future Supreme Court Justice Felix Frankfurter, urging him to accept a position with the Agricultural Adjustment Administration (AAA), one of President Theodore Roosevelt's New Deal programs designed to help farmers devastated by the Great Depression. Hiss left private practice to work for the government. His specialty became defending the constitutionality of Roosevelt's New Deal reforms. Hiss eventually joined the Justice Department as special assistant to the solicitor general to help defend the AAA before the Supreme Court.

In 1936, Hiss joined the State Department. As deputy director of the department's Office of Special Political Affairs, he was in charge of setting up the United Nations. In that capacity, he headed the Dumbarton Oaks Conference, which formally drew up the U.N. Charter.

In the 1970s, FBI documents were made public that indicated the government had withheld information that may have exonerated Hiss. His request to have his conviction overturned was denied, but he was reinstated by the Massachusetts bar in 1975.

Alger Hiss, an American statesman, was accused of espionage and sentenced to prison.

In 1945, Hiss was Secretary General of the San Francisco Conference that organized the United Nations. After the conference he was asked to fly the new U.N. charter back to Washington in a special plane for President Harry S Truman's signature. It was the professional highlight of his life, but he didn't let it go to his head.

"That was the day," Hiss commented later, "when I realized exactly how important I really was—the charter had a parachute and I didn't."[1]

Hiss left government service in 1946. He was President of the Carnegie Endowment for International Peace when, two years later, *Time* magazine editor and former communist Whittaker Chambers publicly accused several government employees, including Hiss, of having been spies in the late 1930s. Hiss vehemently denied the charge and requested to testify before the committee so that he could deny the charges under oath. After Chambers repeated the charge on a radio news program, Hiss also filed a libel suit against Chambers.

In turn, Chambers produced copies of State Department documents he claimed were given to him by Hiss for transmission to the Soviet Union. Hiss denied having typed the copies, and accused Chambers of setting him up. Because the alleged offense had taken place in 1938, the statute of limitations for espionage had passed. But based on Chambers' documentation and testimony, perjury charges were brought against Hiss for having denied before a grand jury that he was a spy. The first trial in 1949 ended in a hung jury, but the second ended with Hiss convicted of perjury. Before being sentenced, Hiss maintained his innocence.

"I would like to thank your Honor for this opportunity again to deny the charges that have been made against me. I want only to add that I am confident that in the future the full facts of how Whittaker Chambers was able to carry out forgery by typewriter will be disclosed. Thank you."[2]

Hiss was sentenced to five years in prison and served forty-four months. To this day, there is controversy as to whether Hiss was truly a spy or a victim of the anticommunist hysteria. There is similar disagreement over the guilt or innocence of Ethel and Julius Rosenberg, who were charged with espionage in 1950 for allegedly handing over atomic bomb information to the Soviets. Ironically, at the time the Soviets were America's allies. The Rosenbergs were implicated by Ethel's brother, David Greenglass, who admitted his guilt in exchange for a lighter sentence. Greenglass had been a soldier assigned to the Los Alamos lab where the atomic bomb was being developed under the direction of Robert Oppenheimer, who would later also come under HUAC scrutiny.

Ethel and Julius, along with co-conspirator Morton Sobell, were convicted of espionage in 1951. It wasn't their conviction that caused the ensuing controversy as much as the sentences: Sobell received thirty years in prison, with a judicial recommendation that he serve the full term. The Rosenbergs received the death penalty. To many, the punishment outweighed the crime. Before and since, others have been found guilty of leaks that were far more damaging to U.S. national security and were not sentenced to die. But the Rosenbergs had the misfortune of being convicted when the country was in the grip of Cold War fear, and they paid the ultimate price as a result. It was in this atmosphere that Senator Joseph McCarthy saw an opportunity to make a name for himself by riding the wave of national paranoia.

When Judge Irving Kaufman sentenced the Rosenbergs to die, he called their crime worse than murder and essentially blamed them for the Korean War. Many historians feel the Rosenbergs were victims of the anti-communist hysteria stirred up by McCarthy.

Julius and Ethel Rosenberg leave the U.S. District Court House after being found guilty of espionage.

In 1946, a House of Representatives committee prepared a list of State Department employees who were allegedly either members of the Communist Party or associated with members of the Communist Party. Because of the growing tension between the Soviets and the Americans, there was genuine concern about where people were placing their loyalty. The committee contacted the State Department demanding to know why communists were allowed to be on the government payroll. State Department officials responded by informing the committee that many of the people had been dismissed or exonerated. The fifty-seven remaining investigations were pending. By 1950, the list was old news—but McCarthy made it newsworthy.

On February 9, during a speech in Wheeling, West Virginia, during a Lincoln Days celebration, McCarthy dramatically held up a list he claimed contained the names of 205 communists who had infiltrated the State Department. He declared, "While I cannot take the time to name all of the men in the State Department who have been named as members of the Communist

As McCarthy's attacks on citizens became more outrageous, his tactics came under criticism. Political cartoonist Herbert Block suggested in this cartoon that McCarthy's charges against the U.S. Army were based on false accusations.

Party and members of a spy ring, I have here in my hand a list of two-hundred and five that were known to the Secretary of State as being members of the Communist Party and who nevertheless are still working and shaping the policy of the State Department."[3]

The press immediately picked up on the charge, and nearly overnight the obscure junior Senator from Wisconsin was known to everybody. It became his mission to expose communists—real or imagined.

J. Robert Oppenheimer is known as the father of the atomic bomb. Considered one of America's top theoretical physicists, during World War II he was named the scientific director of the top secret Manhattan Project at Los Alamos National Laboratory in New Mexico. The Manhattan Project was the government code name for the development and design of a nuclear weapon. After the bombs had been dropped on Hiroshima and Nagasaki, the enormity of what had been developed troubled Oppenheimer, who admitted to President Truman in 1946, "I have blood on my hands."[4]

J. Robert Oppenheimer

Later, it was revealed that during his entire tenure as Manhattan Project director, Oppenheimer had been under investigation by the FBI. In 1936, he had become romantically involved with a Stanford graduate student named Jean Tatlock, who was a member of the Communist Party and who had introduced Oppenheimer to radical politics. But he was never a member of the Communist Party, and his involvement was limited to donating money to liberal causes, such as to the Loyalists in the Spanish Civil War. Robert and Jean eventually broke up, and he married Kitty Harrison in 1940.

Even so, he was followed by U.S. Army security agents during an unannounced trip to California in 1943 to meet Tatlock, who suffered from depression. (She would commit suicide a year later.) Although many considered his actions and past associations suspicious, he was considered essential to the Manhattan Project and no action was taken.

After the war was a different story. Oppenheimer was appointed chairman of the General Advisory Committee of the Atomic Energy Commission, which in 1949 debated the viability of building a thermonuclear bomb, or super atomic bomb. Oppenheimer and the other scientists worried that such a nuclear weapon could lead to the annihilation of the human race. Government officials, however, opted to go forward.

Oppenheimer's reservations about the thermonuclear bomb project called his loyalty into question. In 1953, during the height of McCarthy's anticommunism hysteria, the Atomic Energy Commission stripped Oppenheimer of his security clearance and ousted him from the commission. It also silenced a respected opponent of nuclear proliferation.

McCarthy casts his vote on November

Even though
McCarthy's tactics
were raising increasing
concerns among other
senators, McCarthy
was reelected to the
Senate that year.

Censure

In his speech at Wheeling, West Virginia, McCarthy equated communism to godlessness. "Ladies and gentlemen, can there be anyone tonight who is so blind as to say that the war is not on? Can there be anyone who fails to realize that the Communist world has said the time is now—that this is the time for the show-down between the democratic Christian world and the communistic atheistic world? . . . Unless we face this fact, we shall pay the price that must be paid by those who wait too long."

McCarthy also used his alleged list to attack President Truman's Democratic administration. He singled out Secretary of State Dean Acheson as a communist sympathizer because of his refusal to condemn Alger Hiss.

"As you know," McCarthy continued, "very recently the Secretary of State proclaimed his loyalty to a man guilty of what has always been considered as the most abominable of all crimes—being a traitor to the people who gave him a position of great trust—high treason. . . . He has lighted the spark which is resulting in a moral uprising and will end only when the whole sorry mess of twisted, warped thinkers are swept from the national scene so that we may have a new birth of honesty and decency in government."[1]

McCarthy warned that the very existence of America as people knew it was at stake. "When a great democracy is destroyed it will not be from enemies without but rather because of enemies from within."[2]

Although McCarthy had offered no proof to support his claims of widespread infiltration by communists, the charges struck a nerve and he basked in his newfound notoriety. On February 11, he confronted President Truman, now claiming that he knew of 300 people who were supposed to be discharged from government service because of their communist ties, but saying only 80 had been dismissed. He demanded that Truman order Acheson to give

President Harry S. Truman served as president of the United States from 1945 to 1953.

After President Truman relieved General Douglas MacArthur from leading the United Nations forces in Korea, McCarthy said Truman should be impeached. Truman later was criticized for not doing more to rein in McCarthy's tactics.

Congress "the names and a complete report on all of those who were placed in the Department by Alger Hiss" and that the president "promptly revoke the order in which you provided under no circumstances could a congressional committee obtain any information or help in exposing Communists."[3]

On February 20, 1950, McCarthy gave a six-hour speech on the floor of the Senate about the communist problem, although he backtracked from his earlier pronouncements and claimed he had proof of only 81 communists at the State Department. Never did McCarthy make his list public.

Several Republican senators were disturbed by McCarthy's tactics of making accusations without proof. In June 1950, Senator Margaret Chase Smith of Maine and six other fellow Republicans issued a "Declaration of Conscience" to President Truman. It read, in part:

> As a United States Senator, I am not proud of the way in which the Senate has been made a publicity platform for irresponsible sensationalism. . . . I don't like the way the Senate has been made

a rendezvous for vilification, for selfish political gain at the sacrifice of individual reputations and national unity. I am not proud of the way we smear outsiders from the Floor of the Senate and hide behind the cloak of congressional immunity. . . .

The American people are sick and tired of being afraid to speak their minds lest they be politically smeared as "Communists" or "Fascists" by their opponents. . . . The American people are sick and tired of seeing . . . innocent people smeared.[4]

People outside of government also began to openly question McCarthy's motives. Arthur Miller's 1953 play *The Crucible*, about the Salem witch trials, was an allegory for McCarthy's political witch hunts. Cartoonist Walt Kelly created a menacing character representing McCarthy in his *Pogo* comic strip. But no amount of criticism tempered McCarthy's single-minded cause.

Supporters of McCarthy, then and now, stress that while he was inarguably ambitious and craved fame and attention, he also had rational and reasonable grounds to be concerned about communism. During World War II and after, there had been spies in the U.S. government, as there had been in Britain and other Allied countries. At the same time, the U.S. had its own spies infiltrating the Soviets. Therefore, it was a time of mistrust and uncertainty. The issue for McCarthy detractors wasn't his concerns about spies and disloyalty; it was that McCarthy accused people without any proof, and largely did it out of political partisanship or to generate more headlines for himself.

Despite the growing opposition to McCarthy's communist obsession, Congress passed the Internal Security Act, which required the registration of communist organizations. Members of these groups could not become citizens. It also established the Subversive Activities Control Board to investigate anyone suspected of engaging in "un-American" activities. Truman vetoed the bill, calling it a danger to the First Amendment freedoms of speech, press, and assembly. Congress overrode his veto and the bill became law.

In 1951, the second series of HUAC hearings began, but this time with McCarthy at the helm. He used his powers of subpoena to bring some of the most prominent celebrities of the day, including actress Lucille Ball and writer Dashiell Hammett, before Congress, demanding they name names.

After being reelected in 1952, McCarthy became chairman of the Permanent Investigations Subcommittee and used his powerful position to launch investigations of government officials and agencies. Nobody was safe from McCarthy's suspicions. He publicly questioned the loyalty and integrity of respected people, including Army General George C. Marshall, who won the Nobel Peace Prize in 1953, and even Republican President Dwight D. Eisenhower.

Even more than his outrageous accusations, it was McCarthy's overly aggressive style that made him appear ever more out of control to the general public. He didn't question witnesses so much as he bullied them. His reckless insinuations, seldom backed by proof or fact, ruined many careers. McCarthy's name became synonymous with unsubstantiated, paranoiac character attacks.

One of those attacks, against U.S. Air Force reserve lieutenant Milo Radulovich, helped turn the tide against McCarthy and his anticommunist

To please her beloved grandfather, Lucille Ball registered as a communist in 1936, although she was never an active member.

In 1953, the actress was subpoenaed by HUAC, while I Love Lucy was the most popular show on television. She disavowed any political allegiance to communism and suffered no harm to her career.

People from all walks of life were called to testify by HUAC.

Jackie Robinson, the first African American to play Major League Baseball, denied that blacks in general were pro-communist. He also pointed out that racism against blacks in America was a reality and not just Soviet propaganda.

paranoia. Radulovich had been discharged as a security risk because his sister and father had read what was determined to be subversive newspapers. Based on that, it was determined that members of the Radulovich family were communist sympathizers, and Milo's military career was terminated when he refused to cut ties with them.

Radulovich's discharge was turned into national news in 1953 when CBS reporter Edward R. Murrow, at the time the most respected broadcast journalist in the country, devoted an entire broadcast of the newsmagazine *See It Now* to Radulovich. During the broadcast, Murrow stressed that Radulovich's civil liberties were being trampled, and that he should not be charged with the alleged and unproved offenses of his family. "We believe that the son shall not bear the iniquity of the father, even though that iniquity be proved, and in this case it was not," Murrow said.[5]

Murrow's show also forced Americans to face the harm being inflicted on citizens who had never broken any law. Thousands of viewers wrote to CBS, nearly all voicing support of Radulovich. Newspapers across the country rallied to his defense. Eventually, the U.S. Air Force bowed to the pressure and reinstated Radulovich. The political persecution of Radulovich convinced Murrow that McCarthy was dangerous. On March 9, 1954, Murrow's *See It Now* focused on McCarthy, exposing his tactics. Murrow challenged Americans not to let fear trample their civil rights, saying:

> [T]he line between investigating and persecuting is a very fine one and the junior senator from Wisconsin has stepped over it repeatedly. . . . We must remember always that accusation is not proof and that conviction depends upon evidence and due process of law. We will not walk in fear, one of another. We will not be driven by fear into an age of unreason. . . . [W]e are not descended from fearful men—not from men who feared to write, to speak, to associate, and to defend causes that were, for the moment, unpopular. This is no time for men who oppose Senator McCarthy's methods to keep silent.[6]

Not only was McCarthy under fire from Murrow, but the military had turned against him as well. A year earlier, in 1953, McCarthy had initiated an investigation of espionage within the military. The resulting Army-McCarthy hearings were televised in 1954, and the live broadcasts exposed McCarthy's intimidation tactics and uncertain grasp of the facts. He came across as not merely irresponsible but dishonest and dangerous.

Military leaders openly challenged McCarthy's assertions that high-ranking officers were protecting known communists who had infiltrated the army. Instead, they accused McCarthy of allowing his staff members to blackmail the army by threatening investigations in order to get preferential treatment for his close friend G. David Schine, who had been drafted in 1953.

With public support for McCarthy plummeting, a Senate resolution to strip McCarthy of his committee chairmanship was introduced, and an investigation into McCarthy's tactics, led by Utah Senator Arthur Watkins, was initiated. In December 1954, the Senate passed an official censure of McCarthy for conduct unbecoming to a senator. The vote was 67-22.

He reacted with typical defiance, calling Watkins's committee "the unwitting handmaiden of the Communist Party" and a "lynch party."[7] The reality

was, Joseph McCarthy's political career was over. The obsession with communism that brought him to power ultimately led to his downfall—but not before he had persecuted thousands of innocent people, destroying over an estimated 10,000 careers in the process. Although the most famous victims of McCarthyism were those blacklisted in Hollywood, the vast majority were average citizens. For example, according to the book *Many Are the Crimes: McCarthyism in America*, nearly 3,000 maritime workers and longshoremen lost their jobs.[8]

"YOU MEAN I'M SUPPOSED TO STAND ON THAT?"

In a 1969 interview, General Ralph Zwicker, who had been targeted during the army hearings, admitted that prior to his own run-in with McCarthy, "I was not unsympathetic with the senator. . . . But then I was rapidly disillusioned. He was an opportunist who happened to stumble onto an idea. He climbed a political horse and rode it to death, his own included."[9]

Already a heavy drinker, the censure drove McCarthy into the depths of despair and alcoholism. He died two and a half years later, on May 2, 1957, from cirrhosis of the liver. He was just forty-eight years old. Whether he was a power-hungry opportunist or a misguided, overzealous patriot continues to be debated.

As the public turned against McCarthy, other Republicans also distanced themselves from him, as suggested by this Herbert Block political cartoon.

His motives notwithstanding, McCarthy's attacks against ordinary citizens had a chilling effect on the right of political dissent. Many feared that any criticism of the government might be construed as being unpatriotic and bring possible scrutiny. It is a dilemma that continues—in the wake of the 9/11 terrorist attacks on the United States, anyone who criticized the subsequent war in Iraq or the Patriot Act were seen by some as un-American. The McCarthy Era taught U.S. citizens the importance of constant vigilance to prevent fear from being used as a means to take away constitutionally guaranteed freedoms.

At the height of his career, Edward R. Murrow was the most famous newsman in America. He is also credited with founding the television newsmagazine format. But he is probably best remembered for helping end McCarthy's reign of power.

Murrow was born Egbert Roscoe Murrow in North Carolina on April 25, 1908. When he was six, his family moved to Washington state for a year so that his father could look for work in the lumber industry. They returned to North Carolina, then moved back to Washington for good in 1925. Murrow began college the following year, attending Leland Stanford University, the University of Washington, and Washington State College, majoring in speech. While at Washington State College, he was elected class president and was named top ROTC cadet. He

Edward R. Murrow

also convinced the newly established Columbia Broadcasting Service—CBS—to air a radio program called *A University of the Air*. Even then his skill as a reporter was evident: He managed to get famous personalities like Albert Einstein and German president Paul von Hindenburg to speak on the show. When he graduated, he adopted the first name Edward instead of Egbert.

In 1935, Murrow was hired by CBS as Director of Talks and Education. His first national exposure came during World War II as a war correspondent in Europe,

Milo Radulovich in 1953

during which his signature sign-off, "Good night, and good luck," became a catchphrase. When he returned to New York after the war, he was promoted to Vice President of News, Education, and Discussion Programs. In 1949 he was elected a director of CBS. In the 1950s, Murrow produced the radio program *Hear It Now*. With the success of that program, he took the format to television as *See It Now*. The television show won many awards, including an Emmy and a Peabody Award for the episode spotlighting McCarthy.

Murrow set the standard for broadcast journalism and yet, by the late 1950s, as TV became the dominant entertainment and pop culture medium, that standard became seen as outdated and patronizing. He got out of broadcasting when President John F. Kennedy appointed him to head the U.S. Information Agency, a post he held for three years. Murrow died in New York on April 27, 1965.

Chapter Notes

Chapter One. The Hollywood Ten

1. Jeff Bradley, "The Arts and McCarthyism," *The Denver Post*, July 14, 1989.

2. Griffin Fariello, *Red Scare: Memories of the American Inquisition, an Oral History* (New York: W.W. Norton, 1995), p. 260.

3. CNN.com: "The Cold War: Sinews of Peace," *Iron Curtain*, http://www.cnn.com/SPECIALS/cold.war/episodes/02/documents/churchill

4. Newseum: "The Iron Curtain," http://www.newseum.org/cybernewseum/exhibits/berlin_wall/iron.htm

Chapter Two. Early Years

1. Fred J. Cook, *The Nightmare Decade: The Life and Times of Senator Joe McCarthy* (Random House: New York, 1971), p. 78.

2. Ibid., p. 79.

3. Ibid.

4. Wisconsin Court System, History of the Courts http://www.wicourts.gov/about/organization/history/index.htm

Chapter Three. Political Ambitions

1. Fred J. Cook, *The Nightmare Decade: The Life and Times of Senator Joe McCarthy* (Random House: New York, 1971), p. 83.

2. *State v. McCarthy*, 255 Wis. 234, 38 N.W.2d 679 (1949).

3. *Joseph R. McCarthy and the Senate* (Amherst: University of Massachusetts Press, 1987), p. 5.

Chapter Four. National Exposure

1. The Alger Hiss Story: Search for the Truth http://homepages.nyu.edu/~th15/who.html

2. Denise Noe, Court TV, *The Alger Hiss Case* http://www.crimelibrary.com/terrorists_spies/spies/hiss/10.html

3. Richard Rovere, *Senator Joe McCarthy* (New York: Meridian, 1960), p. 125.

4. NuclearFiles.com, "The Oppenheimer Affair." http://www.nuclearfiles.org/menu/key-issues/nuclear-weapons/history/cold-war/oppenheimer-affair/oppenheimer-affair-intro.htm

Chapter Five. Censure

1. Enemies from Within; Senator Joseph R. McCarthy's Accusations of Disloyalty http://historymatters.gmu.edu/d/6456

2. Ibid.

3. Ibid.

4. American Rhetoric: Top 100 Speeches—Margaret Chase Smith, "Declaration of Conscience" http://www.americanrhetoric.com/speeches/margaretchasesmithconscience.html

5. CBSNews.com, "Remembering Milo Radulovich," November 20, 2007, http://www.cbsnews.com/stories/2007/11/20/eveningnews/main3528798.shtml

6. Michael Jay Friedman, "See It Now": Murrow vs. McCarthy, http://usinfo.state.gov/products/pubs/murrow/friedman.htm

7. BBC News: On This Day, December 2—"1954: U.S. Senate Condemns McCarthy," http://news.bbc.co.uk/onthisday/hi/dates/stories/december/2/newsid_3205000/3205423.stm

8. Ellen Schrecker, *Many Are the Crimes: McCarthyism in America* (New York: Little, Brown, 1998), p. 267.

9. New York Times News Service, "General Hounded by McCarthy," *Chicago Tribune*, August 12, 1991, Chicagoland, p. 7.

Chronology

1908   Joseph Raymond McCarthy is born on a farm in Outagamie County, Wisconsin, on November 14.

1922   At the age of fourteen, he drops out of school.

1927   Joe enters high school at age nineteen.

1928   McCarthy earns high school diploma.

1930   He enrolls at Marquette University in Milwaukee, Wisconsin.

1936   He runs for district attorney but is defeated.

1939   McCarthy is elected circuit court judge.

1942   He leaves the bench and joins the U.S. Marine Corps as a first lieutenant.

1944   He loses his first run for the U.S. Senate.

1945   He is honorably discharged from the Marines with the rank of captain.

1946   McCarthy is elected to the U.S. Senate over a Democratic opponent by a 2:1 margin.

1947   The first HUAC hearings take place; Hollywood Ten are blacklisted.

1950   In February, McCarthy claims that the U.S. State Department has been infiltrated by Communists. The Tydings Committee hearings dispute these accusations.

1951   McCarthy leads second round of HUAC hearings.

1952   He is reelected to the U.S. Senate.

1953   The Senate's Hennings Report cites McCarthy for unethical, but not illegal, behavior.

1953   McCarthy investigates the Army Signal Corps. Edward R. Murrow's coverage of the Radulovich trial marks the turning point in McCarthy's popularity.

1954   McCarthy accuses Secretary of the Army Robert T. Stevens of concealing foreign espionage activities. McCarthy is censured by the Senate.

1957   He dies of complications from cirrhosis of the liver, brought on by alcoholism, on May 2.

2003   Senate records from McCarthy's Committee on Government Operations are made public.

2008   New revelations by convicted spy Morton Sobell indicate that the Rosenbergs and Alger Hiss were guilty of spying.

Timeline in History

1848   Karl Marx publishes *Communist Manifesto*.

1914   Assassination of Austria's Archduke Franz Ferdinand leads to World War I.

1917   Czar Nicholas II is overthrown by the Bolsheviks.

1924   Stalin becomes leader of Soviet Union.

1928   State courts in Washington rule that Workers Party candidates may appear on ballots.

1939   American Communist Party membership peaks at 100,000.

1948   Communist takeover in Czechoslovakia occurs in February.

1949   China is taken over by communist leader, Mao Ze-dong.

1951   General Douglas MacArthur is removed from command for insubordination.

1955   Warsaw Pact is signed.

1959   Communist leader Fidel Castro takes over Cuba.

1961   Bay of Pigs, the attempted overthrow of Castro, begins in April; it fails.

1962   The Cuban Missile Crisis nearly brings the United States and the Soviet Union to nuclear war.

1968   Soviets crush Prague Spring by occupying Czechoslovakia.

1969   Under pressure from California governor Ronald Reagan, the University of California fires Angela Davis because of her ties to the Communist Party.

1975   Cambodia's Khmer Rouge Communists overthrow the government.

1980   The United States boycotts the Moscow Olympics to protest the Soviet invasion of Afghanistan.

1989   Berlin Wall falls.

1991   Break-up of the Soviet Union begins.

1997   Britain turns control of Hong Kong over to China.

2008   North Korea agrees to discuss nuclear disarmament.

Further Reading

For Young Readers

Brooks, Philip. *The McCarthy Hearings*, Chicago: Heinemann Library, 2003.

Sherrow, Victoria. *Joseph McCarthy and the Cold War*. Farmington Hills, Mich.: Blackbirch Press, 2001.

Wicker, Tom. *Shooting Star: The Brief Arc of Joe McCarthy*. New York: Harcourt, 2006.

Works Consulted

Bradley, Jeff. "The Arts and McCarthyism." *The Denver Post*, July 14, 1989.

Cook, Fred J. *The Nightmare Decade: The Life and Times of Senator Joe McCarthy*. New York: Random House, 1971.

Fariello, Griffin. *Red Scare: Memories of the American Inquisition, an Oral History*. New York: W. W. Norton, 1995.

Griffith, Robert. *The Politics of Fear: Joseph R. McCarthy and the Senate*. Amherst: University of Massachusetts Press, 1987.

New York Times News Service. "General Hounded by McCarthy." *Chicago Tribune*, August 12, 1991, Chicagoland, p. 7.

Oshinsky, David M. *A Conspiracy So Immense: The World of Joe McCarthy*. New York: Oxford University Press, 2005.

Stolberg, Sheryl Gay. "Transcripts Detail Secret Questioning in '50s by McCarthy." *New York Times*, May 6, 2003.

On the Internet

"After the Purge." *The Guardian*, August 9, 2005, p. G6 http://www.guardian.co.uk/film/2005/aug/09/features.features11

The Alger Hiss Story: Search for the Truth http://homepages.nyu.edu/~th15/who.html

American Rhetoric: Top 100 Speeches—Margaret Chase Smith, "Declaration of Conscience" http://www.americanrhetoric.com/speeches/margaretchasesmithconscience.html

BBC News: On This Day, December 2—"1954: U.S. Senate Condemns McCarthy" http://news.bbc.co.uk/onthisday/hi/dates/stories/december/2/newsid_3205000/3205423.stm

CNN.com: "The Cold War: Sinews of Peace," Iron Curtain, http://www.cnn.com/SPECIALS/cold.war/episodes/02/documents/churchill

Enemies from Within: "Senator Joseph R. McCarthy's Accusations of Disloyalty" http://historymatters.gmu.edu/d/6456

FBI, Joseph McCarthy http://foia.fbi.gov/foiaindex/mccarthy.htm

HUAC (House Un-American Activities Committee) http://www.fsm-a.org/stacks/AP_files/APHUAC60.html

Marquette University Library, Special Collections, Joseph R. McCarthy Papers http://www.marquette.edu/library/collections/archives/Mss/JRM/mss-JRM.html

Noe, Denise. *Court TV*, The Alger Hiss Case http://www.crimelibrary.com/terrorists_spies/spies/hiss/10.html

Glossary

blacklist
To name as someone to be avoided, especially for employment.

censure (SEN-chur)
A formal reprimand.

Cold War
The conflict between the United States and the Soviet Union over ideas that stopped just short of actual violence.

communism (KAH-myoo-nih-zum)
A political system in which all citizens share equally; a government controlled by a single authority.

iniquity (in-IH-kwih-tee)
A gross injustice; wickedness; a sin.

innuendo (in-yoo-EN-doh)
An insinuation or suggestion.

jurisdiction (jur-is-DIK-shun)
The power to apply the law; the geographical area of legal authority.

litigation (lih-tih-GAY-shun)
A legal proceeding; a lawsuit.

maverick (MAA-vrik)
An independent thinker; someone who does not follow expected behavior.

propaganda (prah-puh-GAN-duh)
One-sided information intended to change opinion.

radical (RAA-dih-kul)
Promoting extreme changes to existing laws or customs.

ROTC
Reserve Officers' Training Corps, a division of the armed forces that trains college-educated recruits to become officers in the military.

statute (STAA-chewt)
A law enacted by legislators.

subpoena (sub-PEE-nuh)
An official summons to appear before a court.

subversive (sub-VER-siv)
Promoting ideas that could undermine or overthrow a government.

Index